n Emerald Diamond Paper or Plastic Cotton or Calico Leather Silk, or Fruit and Flo
ery Aluminium or Tin Steel Linen Lace Jewellery Glass or Crystal China Silver
ilk, or Fruit and Flowers Wooden Iron or Sugar Woollen Bronze, Rubber, Salt or Elec
l China Silver Pearl Coral Ruby Sapphire Golden Emerald Diamond Paper or P
e, Rubber, Salt or Electrical Appliances Copper or Pottery Aluminium or Tin Steel I
Diamond Paper or Plastic Cotton or Calico Leather Silk, or Fruit and Flowers Wo
nium or Tin Steel Linen Lace Jewellery Glass or Crystal China Silver Pearl Coral
and Flowers Wooden Iron or Sugar Woollen Bronze, Rubber, Salt or Electrical Applia
ilver Pearl Coral Ruby Sapphire Golden Emerald Diamond Paper or Plastic Cotto
lt or Electrical Appliances Copper or Pottery Aluminium or Tin Steel Linen Lace Jewe
er or Plastic Cotton or Calico Leather Silk, or Fruit and Flowers Wooden Iron or S
Steel Linen Lace Jewellery Glass or Crystal China Silver Pearl Coral Ruby Sap
ers Wooden Iron or Sugar Woollen Bronze, Rubber, Salt or Electrical Appliances Co
arl Coral Ruby Sapphire Golden Emerald Diamond Paper or Plastic Cotton or C
ectrical Appliances Copper or Pottery Aluminium or Tin Steel Linen Lace Jewellery
astic Cotton or Calico Leather Silk, or Fruit and Flowers Wooden Iron or Sugar Wo
nen Lace Jewellery Glass or Crystal China Silver Pearl Coral Ruby Sapphire Go
len Iron or Sugar Woollen Bronze, Rubber, Salt or Electrical Appliances Copper or Po
by Sapphire Golden Emerald Diamond Paper or Plastic Cotton or Calico Leather
ances Copper or Pottery Aluminium or Tin Steel Linen Lace Jewellery Glass or Cr
on or Calico Leather Silk, or Fruit a   Sugar Woollen Bro
Jewellery Glass or Crystal China S   Golden Em
Sugar Woollen Bronze, Rubber, Salt   ottery Alumin
ire Golden Emerald Diamond Paper or Plastic   ther Silk, or
opper or Pottery Aluminium or Tin Steel Linen Lace Jewellery Glass or Crystal C

THE
BOOK OF
Anniversaries

THE BOOK OF ANNIVERSARIES

Loving Ways to Celebrate Your Marriage

DR R. BRASCH

Angus&Robertson

An imprint of HarperCollins*Publishers*

CONTENTS

THE ANNIVERSARY LIST

PREFACE

The Book of Anniversaries is for couples celebrating the anniversary of that special day when they became husband and wife.

It gives and explains the choice of anniversary names, and suggests a variety of meaningful ways in which to commemorate these special days, along with many helpful suggestions for appropriate gifts.

Remember, observations linked with a specific anniversary because of its name may apply just as well to other anniversaries, so you may find food for thought right throughout the book. The selection of gifts is meant merely as a guide. Most importantly, they should relate to the recipient's individual taste and pursuits. The choice also depends on whether the present is meant for one's partner or for another couple. Of course, any type of thoughtfully chosen present will be welcome — not least because the increase of years is reflected by ever more valuable materials, such as rubies and diamonds!

■ How the Anniversaries Were Named

Up until medieval times, wedding anniversaries had no special names. They were just described in terms of the number of years that had passed since the wedding day. Then the custom arose in central Europe of giving distinction to the 25th and 50th anniversaries. To celebrate them, the husband crowned his wife with a wreath, made from silver or gold respectively. Though this practice has become obsolete, it survives in the description of those special days as 'silver' and 'golden' anniversaries.

The names of all the other anniversaries are of much more modern origin. They were primarily suggested by different gifts which became linked with each specific anniversary. To meet contemporary and local conditions and technological advances, some of the categories have been changed or updated. For instance, in view of modern ecological awareness and conservation, the original present of ivory for the 14th anniversary has been replaced with one of jewellery.

The range of presents extends from objects made from paper for the first anniversary to a gift of diamonds for the 60th or 75th one. However, the sequence does not necessarily reflect the durability or 'value' of the different anniversaries; rather, each symbolises a certain aspect of the couple's relationship at or around that time.

Gifts should always be personal. They need not be expensive or extravagant, but they should come from the heart. A simple note might be treasured more than a costly present.

A touching example is that of Henry George, the renowned economist and social reformer. The occasion was not an actual wedding anniversary, but the anniversary of the day he first met the girl he was going to marry. On the 13th of October, 1883, she woke to find this note on her bedside table which Henry had written and left for her:

"For 23 years we have been closer to each other than to anyone else in the world, and I think we esteem each other more and love each other better than when we first began to love. You are now 'fat, fair and forty', and to me the mature woman is handsomer and more lovable than the slip of a girl whom 23 years ago I met without knowing that my life was to be bound up with hers. We are not rich — so poor just now, in fact,
that all I can give you on this anniversary is a little love-letter — but there is no one we can afford to envy, and in each other's love we have what no wealth could compensate for. And so let us go, true and loving, trusting in Him to carry us farther who has brought us so far with so little to regret."

A lasting, loving partnership is indeed a cause for celebration in a world filled with turmoil and constant change, where so many factors seem to be threatening the stability of our lives.

I am my beloved's, and
my beloved is mine.
Song of Songs 6,3

■ The Celebration

To a happily married couple, no date is more joyous than the anniversary of their wedding day, no matter how many years have passed since they were handed that certificate which pronounced them husband and wife. The wedding anniversary date should always be kept free for celebrating and it should be the first date to be entered into one's diary at the beginning of each year.

Apart from a gift, which may be linked with the designation of the day, the wedding anniversary may be celebrated in a variety of other ways. Some couples may send each other traditional greeting cards, their text and ornamentation thoughtfully chosen to suit the partner's taste. Others might actually make or draw their own very personal cards to express their special feelings in simple and genuine language — though perhaps words may prove inadequate.

To confine the celebration to a card or a note, however, would be the very least to be expected! An anniversary is a special occasion and should be marked by something additional. Some couples prefer to celebrate their anniversary on their own, while others may enjoy doing so in the midst of family and friends. A festive dinner at home or at a favourite restaurant could become an annual tradition. For the music lover, how about a visit to a concert? Or, for those who appreciate theatre, perhaps a show could highlight the day. Revisiting some place from their courting days will give a couple precious time for happy remembrances and may also serve as an opportunity for jointly planning the year ahead. And, to the religiously motivated, a joint prayer of thanksgiving or attending worship may be most appropriate.

Life has its ups and downs. When a couple reminisce on their anniversary, they recall both trivial and difficult times. This might include moments when harsh words were spoken or when a disagreement spoilt a day. However, recalling even the unhappy times need not interfere with the enjoyment of the celebration: on the contrary, it will make the couple realise that such upsets, in retrospect, were really insignificant. Now that they are relegated to the past, those incidents can be seen to have deepened their relationship, making it firmer and more mature.

∎ The Missing Rib

According to Biblical tradition, woman was created from one of man's ribs. Ever since, it has been said, men have been running all over the world to find their missing ribs! Some never succeed and become 'confirmed bachelors'. Others get hold of a rib, but it is not theirs; it does not fit and is the cause of much distress.

Fortunate are those who find their 'rib'. It makes them complete. They will have a fulfilling life, with peace in their homes and joy and contentment in their hearts. They can truly count their blessings, and that is exactly what they do when they 'count' the anniversaries since their wedding, happily recalling how many years have passed since the day when — with hope and anticipation — they pledged their love for one another.

Professor Alfred Whitehead was an English mathematician and philosopher of world renown. He realised that, like so many famous figures, he could never have been so successful without his wife's encouragement and support. "By myself I am only one more professor, but with Evelyn I am first-rate," he said fondly.

∎ Marriage Made in Heaven

A happily married couple will say that their marriage was 'made in heaven'.

This romantic claim is actually based on an ancient belief that, when a soul left its heavenly abode and was about to enter an individual's body, the Divine Master had already determined its future partner. For two 'soul mates' to be joined in marriage was, therefore, not the result of a lucky chance. It was truly predestined.

Going back to Roman days, we find the record of a conversation between a matron and a theologian who were discussing God. The lady wanted to know what God had been doing ever since completing the work of creation. He had been arranging marriages, the wise man informed her. This answer did not satisfy the lady. There was no need for divine help to join couples, she argued, it was an easy job. Determined to prove her point she gathered her many slaves together and paired them off ... Well, it did not take long for all those incompatible newlyweds to quarrel with each other! The noble lady had to agree after all that matchmaking was best left to God.

THE Anniver

SARY
List

PAPER

PLASTIC

Of all the anniversaries, the one marking the completion of that first year of marriage is probably the most significant. Though only 12 months have passed, the couple's entire lives have changed. They will have shared both good and bad times, and will have gained a new dimension of sharing in all that they do and experience.

The first year of marriage is one of great enrichment, where the couple can gratefully acknowledge the benefits their union has brought them. It is also a memorable 'milestone' for recognising how they have dealt with the realities of life together.

The excitement of the wedding day, with all its glamour, gifts and promises, is inevitably followed by the cares of everyday life. Each partner should now feel as though they can confront these cares with a devoted helpmate, rather than alone.

The first year will also prove a period of adjustment. After all, bride and groom were used to living independently and, in the majority of cases, to deciding issues on their own. For the first time, they will have learnt to appreciate the value of shared decisions, and to do so in a process of give-and-take. They will also have realised that many tasks, which would have been impossible to achieve alone, can be actioned together.

Some couples might have had to deal with that very common mistake in early married life, of one of the partners trying to change the other to his or her ways! Hopefully, the pair will have come to respect each other's individuality.

This is most often known as the 'paper' anniversary because, on their marriage day, the bride and groom are said to have started a jointly authored book, being given a blank sheet of paper for that first page, as it were. They will have filled it with the story of the very beginning of their shared adventure. May your 'paper' anniversary prove to be merely the introduction to a vast volume about your life together, telling what love can do and accomplish.

Paper might be relatively inexpensive, but we can make it very precious by the way we make use of it. A young married couple may have little wealth, but they can be very rich in their contribution to each other's lives — and that is an 'investment' that can only gain in value as the years go by.

A good marriage is like a handshake.

There is no upper hand.

GIFT SUGGESTIONS

Traditionally, a husband's gift to his wife on their first anniversary was an eternity ring.

Other ideas include:

Personalised notepaper, printed letterheads or visiting cards

A collection of recipes

Buttons

Paper sewing patterns

Tickets for a theatre performance, the ballet or a concert

Drawings or sketches

A scrapbook or photo album

A perpetual calendar

A book or a book voucher

A subscription to a magazine or journal

Monogrammed serviettes, or kitchen or guest towels

Anything from the vast range of plastic goods available may also be suitable, such as:

Playing cards or table games

A garden hose

Kitchen containers

Floral arrangements

2nd Anniversary

Cotton

CALICO

the changes married life brings, the couple's union will have proved strong. Marriage will have

Apart from indicating the type of present to be selected to mark this occasion, the choice of the name 'cotton' lends itself to a variety of symbolic interpretations. For instance:

Cotton is a natural substance. Two years of marriage will have taught the couple the importance of being their natural selves, and of shunning anything artificial in their relationship.

Just as cotton is comfortable to wear, they will have experienced a new feeling of comfort, brought about by being totally relaxed together.

Cotton is a hardy fibre. With all

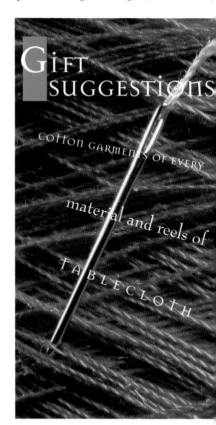

Gift suggestions

cotton garments of every material and reels of tablecloth

given them fortitude, enabling them to overcome any untoward circumstances.

Cotton clings easily to one's clothes. Thus, metaphorically, it symbolises how the husband and wife now cling to each other.

Some couples might worry that once the white heat of passion of the early days has abated, their relationship might cool down too, an analogy suggested by the coolness of cotton fabric. However, they may be reassured by remembering that cotton, if ever smudged or dirtied, can be easily cleaned and restored to its original pristine state.

initialled handcherchiefs

TYPE RANGING FROM SHIRTS AND BLOUSES TO UNDERWEAR AND SOCKS

sewing cotton

towels for the bathroom or beach

AND SERVIETTES

3rd Anniversary

LEATHER

From the earliest days and in many cultures, three has been seen as a lucky number. The Greek philosopher Pythagoras, in the 6th century BC, called it 'the perfect number', and Shakespeare wrote that if there was luck in all odd numbers, it was particularly plentiful in the number 3.

To link the occasion with leather gives it added meaning. Leather reminds us of the power of transformation. Just as humans learnt to change perishable skins into a tough and lasting material, so too can love transform our lives.

apparel
such as a

BELT

jacket

a pair of

SHOES OR SLIPPERS

handbag briefcase purse wallet

OR KEYCASE

Writing set

Silk

Flowers

Fruit

Four years of married life combines a multiplicity of experiences which may explain how this anniversary came to be called by two different names.

Silk expresses elegance and is a fabric that caresses the wearer. We speak of the fruit of one's labour, implying that nothing in life is achieved without effort. One must put into marriage as much as one hopes to get out of it. Flowers have been called love's truest language. 'To say it with flowers' is appropriate at all times, not least so when celebrating four years of a happy marriage.

Gift suggestions

Lingerie or nightwear

A
silk
scarf

BLOUSE OR SHIRT

Tie

or cravat

Dress *or* dress material

BASKET OF FRUIT OR FLOWERS

Plants for the house or garden

5th Anniversary

WOODEN

Through the ages, wood has provided us with shelter, warmth and comfort – all practical considerations in the happy home. The symbolism of wood is important, too. Firstly, it comes from a tree, whose roots are reaching ever deeper into the ground, making it secure enough to endure the stormiest of weather. A tree is also a symbol of growth, each year putting forth blossom and then fruit.

Five years of marriage represent endurance and stability. Also, by the fifth anniversary, many marriages will have been enriched by the birth of at least one child. This event will have completely changed the couple's lives, giving them a new focus and a most rewarding task to be jointly undertaken. Following the birth of children, all subsequent anniversaries will have an added meaning. The growth of the couple's offspring symbolises how their own love story has not come to a standstill, but is an ongoing, exciting process, making their lives ever more worthwhile.

A successful marriage is an edifice that must be rebuilt every day.

André Maurois

Gift Suggestions

GARDEN FURNITURE

Occasional tables

PHOTO
FRAMES

KITCHEN UTENSILS

Wooden spoons

or chopping board

FOR THE BOOKLOVER

shelving or a newspaper rack

IRON | SUGAR

A happy marriage is not merely for two people to gaze lovingly into each other's eyes. It is rather for them to be looking in the same direction, with a common goal in their sight.

GIFT SUGGESTIONS

Decorative objects for the house or garden made from wrought iron

Fireside irons

A year's supply of every type of sugar, such as caster, lump, brown and white, all presented in attractive canisters

7th Anniversary

WOOLLEN

Seven has been regarded as a mystical, if not sacred figure, which in itself completes a circle. As with the 7th day of the week, the 7th year of marriage demands special observance.

Wool is as durable as true love. Love should not be subject to what has become known as the 'seven-year itch', with its accompanying threat to loyalty and fidelity. Wool is also soft to the touch. A loving couple knows how to give each other comfort, even when times are rough.

The days that make us happy make us wise.

John Masefield

Gift suggestions

Woollen garments, such as gloves or socks, or a cap, jumper, cardigan or dressing gown

A decorative throw rug for the house or car

Blankets

A small carpet

BRONZE
RUBBER
SALT
ELECTRICAL
APPLIANCES

No matter which type of gift is chosen, each carries with it a special message, highlighting a particular aspect of a truly successful and fulfilling marriage.

Bronze, which has given its name to an entire period of history, well merits being linked with an anniversary. An alloy, bronze derives its quality from this very combination of a diversity of metals. Two people, with their individualities joined together, become a couple with a fortitude to face life which, singly, they would never possess.

With such a variety of themes for this anniversary, there are many possible gift choices.

GIFT SUGGESTIONS

Different varieties of salt – choose from rock salt, sea salt and garlic salt, for instance – packed into attractive glass jars

An electric power tool or shaver for the husband, a hair dryer or heated rollers for the wife, or a toaster, electric blanket or toothbrushes for both of them to enjoy

An electric can opener, blender or food processor, microwave oven or pressure cooker

RUBBER

kitchen gloves, apron

or

bathmat

Bronze ornament,

platter or

WALL PLAQUE

COPPER POTTERY

GIFT SUGGESTIONS

To be 'on cloud nine' aptly describes the happiness experienced by a couple who complete nine years of marriage.

Among the first metals humans learnt to use, copper was specially treasured because of its malleability. Copper also gives out an atmosphere of warmth, just as affection does. Both respond to loving care: the more they are polished, the more they will shine.

Pottery preceded copper by thousands of years, but both substances share the gift of pliability, so essential in a successful marriage.

Decorative objects made from copper, such as a plate, urn, jug or pot

Choose from many pottery items, from simple bowls to a large sculpture for the garden

10th Anniversary

Aluminium — Tin

Tin is a durable and useful metal; however, it is the symbolism of tin that is most relevant here. Firstly, just as tin is used to preserve food, so has the couple's affection been kept fresh. Secondly, just as the making of a faultless tin requires meticulous workmanship, so staying in love has demanded a thorough cultivation of mutual interests. After 10 years of marriage, a couple can look back proudly on many achievements attained through being true helpmates to each other.

Marriage has been compared to a currency note. Torn in two, neither part is worth anything. Each needs the other to be of value.

GIFT SUGGESTIONS

An ample supply of tinfoil is perhaps the most practical gift

A tin grater, baking tins and a tin opener

Tins of food, particularly if they contain a special treat

STEEL

Steel is one of the most resistant and unyielding of alloys. Steel cables hold up heavy bridges and steel's strength is proverbial. Combined with other elements, it never rusts and defies any attacks of acid.

How appropriate then was the choice of steel for the naming of this anniversary. In eleven years of close togetherness a couple will have acquired indomitable strength against the many vagaries life, with its tensions and irritations, presents.

As your days, so shall be your strength.

Deuteronomy 33, 25

GiFT SUGGESTiONS

Stainless steel cutlery

Tea or coffee pot, or milk jug

Saucepans

Trays

Butter dish, salt and pepper shakers

12th Anniversary

Linen

Gift Suggestions

After 12 years of marriage, much of the wedding or trousseau linen will have probably worn out. Therefore, gifts of sheets, pillowcases, towels, serviettes, tablecloths and hand or guest towels may all be welcomed.

LACE

Lace represents the process in marriage of two lives becoming ever more interwoven, as, through the years, husband and wife jointly create their unique pattern of life with their own distinctive characteristics.

The more care taken in producing the lace, the more precious becomes the fabric. The best of lace has always been the result of painstaking solicitude.

Here is my heart,

It's yours.

I've saved it for you.

　　Beverley Cottee

Gift suggestions

Place mats or a tablecloth

Lace collar or dress

Lace-trimmed handkerchiefs

Curtains

Bedspread

JEWELLERY

From its very beginning, human existence has been enriched by many types of jewellery. Jewellery was valued universally for a vast range of uses.

Whether fashioned by early peoples in the worship of their gods and as a safeguard for their bodies and spirits, or designed by modern superior craftsmanship for personal adornment, throughout the ages and the world, jewellery and gemstones have been treasured as a most precious possession.

GIFT SUGGESTIONS

Naturally for this anniversary jewellery of any kind, from costume jewellery to precious gems, would be appropriate.

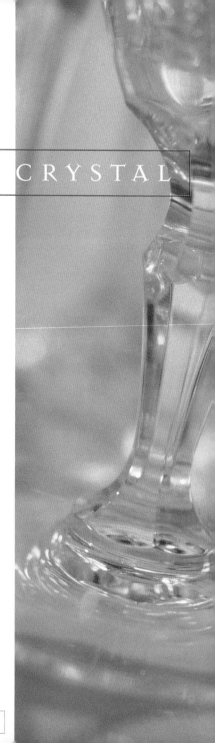

15th Anniversary

GLASS CRYSTAL

A couple will cherish many an object of glass not merely because of its beauty but for the memory it recalls of some special moment during the fifteen years of their union. They may think of the glasses of wine they shared and the toasts that they drank to each other.

Crystal is one of the most valuable types of glass. When tapped, it gives beautiful resonant tones like the sound of true happiness that reverberates in the hearts of a happy couple. May this day be as sparkling as the many-faceted crystal.

Gift
SUGGESTIONS

JUGS

or bowls

PAPERWEIGHTS

Vases and glasses

BOTTLES

(preferably not empty!)

CHINA

China is an apt gift choice for this anniversary. Certainly, after 20 years of marriage, it is likely that quite a few treasured pieces may have been lost or broken.

Apart from this practical consideration, the symbolism of china prompts some thoughtful observations. Just as a precious piece of china gains in value with the passing years so too, after 20 years together, will the couple have enriched each other's lives. And, just as they might be wanting to replenish their china collection at this time, they may also wish to reaffirm their vows for the years to come.

Such appreciation is all the more appropriate in our modern times, when we witness so many marriage break-ups. Perhaps the 'china' anniversary may also serve as a reminder that a marriage may become fragile if care is not taken to preserve it.

The best part of a happy marriage is coming home after a trying day and being able to discuss your woes with an understanding partner.

GIFT SUGGESTIONS

Select from the enormous variety of china objects which may be bought – from ornaments to a dinner service or a special cup – depending on the recipient's taste.

SILVER

Unlike most of the other anniversaries which owe their designation to the type of gift suggested, the naming of this anniversary is linked with a beautiful and romantic tradition. Many years ago, the sharing of twenty-five years of marriage was commemorated by the husband placing a wreath of silver on his wife's head. This act expressed so much more than words could ever say.

Even though the tradition has been abandoned, the naming of the silver anniversary still holds a special magic – the value of a couple's marriage being indeed comparable to the qualities of sterling silver.

Marriage in amity is this world's paradise.

GIFT SUGGESTIONS

Silver platter or tray

TEA OR COFFEE SET

Cutlery

VASE OR JUG

Jewellery
– watch, bracelet, necklace, ring

Cufflinks,
tiepin or tie-tack

30th Anniversary

PEARL

That the 30th wedding anniversary is related to the pearl may be somewhat surprising, given the widespread superstition that pearls are associated with tears (unless they are tears of happiness).

It is, however, in the creation and qualities of the pearl that we find symbolism relevant to a loving relationship spanning 30 years. For instance, a pearl does not immediately attain its full splendour; rather, like marital happiness, it grows with the years. Also, to keep its lustre, pearls have to be worn next to the warmth of the body. In much the same way, marriage needs warmth and affection.

A significant consideration is

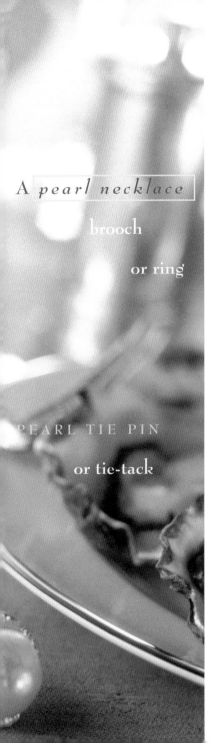

A *pearl necklace*

brooch

or ring

PEARL TIE PIN

or tie-tack

that, in the majority of cases, a pearl grows as the result of an untoward incident in an oyster's life – usually when a grain of sand enters its shell. Metaphorically speaking, after 30 years of marriage, a couple is also bound to have encountered unforeseen 'irritants'. However, if theirs is a mature and loving relationship, such crises may actually enhance the relationship and add value to their lives together.

It occasionally happens that a string of pearls may snap, and the pearls be scattered on the ground. Surely no one would leave them there, preferring instead to collect and restring the pearls, wearing them with even more care in the future. This brings us to another analogy – what of couples who may experience a break-up of their marriage? Perhaps, with wisdom and care, they will similarly gather the broken pieces and repair the damage, so as to restore their relationship to its former beauty.

The only thing that can hallow marriage is love, and the only genuine marriage is that which is hallowed by love.

Leo Tolstoy

35th Anniversary

ORAL

Unique of its kind is the coral. Not a mere gem, coral is an organic substance with a wide range of beautiful colours, so much like a loving relationship.

Coral reefs continuously grow, just as even after thirty-five years of marriage, life has not come to a standstill. The couple, grateful for the dreams that have come true, will talk of all the things they still want to do and the plans they have for the future, making an actuality of many a possibility.

Gift suggestions

Coral ornaments
Necklace, brooch or ring
Tie bar or tie-tack

40th Anniversary

RUBY

There are several reasons to explain the selection of this stone for such an auspicious day. A ruby is, literally, symbolic of a 'red letter day', which an anniversary of 40 years of marriage surely is!

The ruby has been treasured since very ancient times. One legend tells us that it was the ruby which contained the original spark of life. Another superstition was that the ruby was thought to render humans invulnerable. To this end, people actually cut their flesh and inserted rubies, before sewing over the wound. By association, after 40 years of marriage, a husband and wife have become almost one, and they also serve to protect each other.

Rubies were once thought to bestow on their wearer the supernatural gift of being able to sense the unspoken and invisible. Again, this parallels the situation of a husband and wife who, having shared their lives for so long, intuitively understand each other. Another superstition held that an inextinguishable fire burned inside a ruby which nothing could subdue, making this gem an apt symbol for a shared love which has brightened a couple's lives for so long.

The length of time – 40 years – is of interest in itself. From very ancient times, 40 has been considered a magic numeral, and has been associated with many historic events and religious traditions, and even with the preservation of health. It was believed to confer protection – explaining the derivation of our modern word 'quarantine', from the Italian for 'forty', referring in this case to a period of exactly 40 days.

To be happy and lasting, marriage requires not only finding the right partner but being the right partner.

Gift suggestions

Jewellery – brooch, pendant, bracelet or ring

RUBY GLASS BOWL

Ruby glasses

Tie pin or tie-tack

SAPPHIRE

The Persians called the sapphire the celestial stone and not without reason, as its pure blue colour made people link it with the heavens.

Symbolically the stone is said to represent truth and sincerity, the very qualities which ensure lasting and rewarding love.

Life is a succession of lessons which must be lived to be understood.

Emerson

Gift Suggestions

Jewellery — ring, earrings, brooch, necklace or pendant

Tie pin or tie-tack

50th Anniversary

GOLDEN

As with the silver anniversary, this one's name harks back to the time when a husband would honour his wife of 50 years with a wreath, this time a gold one.

GIFT SUGGESTIONS

Gold has long been prized as the most precious of metals. From time immemorial, people have searched for El Dorado, that legendary city said to have been filled with golden treasure. On the occasion of their golden anniversary, a happily married couple can also say that they have found 'treasure'. Think of all the people who, for centuries, have tried to turn base metal into gold. In parallel, a couple who have passed through the 'crucible of life' for 50 years, can take pride in having created 'gold' together.

In Biblical times, a 50th anniversary was described as a jubilee, and was publicly proclaimed with a trumpet fanfare. It is indeed a jubilant event, worthy of celebration with an ever-expanding family of children, grandchildren and perhaps even great-grandchildren.

This anniversary's main sentiment is one of gratitude for the many blessings which have been enjoyed together. That 'book of happiness' referred to in the 'paper' anniversary should now contain many pages, filled with a multitude of moods and events. The couple's continuous striving to make life worthwhile for each other has been successful. Fortunate indeed is the woman whose husband still tells her, on their golden wedding anniversary: "Darling, you are beautiful!"

On the occasion of his 50th wedding anniversary, Henry Ford was asked for his formula for a successful marriage. It was the same principle which had ensured the success of his cars, he explained: "Stick to the one model"!

EMERALD

The emerald was known thousands of years ago and treasured by almost all faiths. Its green colour was a reminder of fertility. According to Pliny, the green of the emerald 'outgreened' even the verdure of nature.

A Moslem tradition serves as perhaps the most apt analogy for the 55th wedding anniversary. It states that the first of the seven heavens was made up of emeralds. Its restful green — the colour of nature — suggested a feeling of perfect relaxation, similar to that attained after these many years of companionship.

GIFT SUGGESTIONS

If affordable, an emerald eternity ring and tie pin or tie-tack would be an excellent choice.

iAMOND

After 60 years of married life, it is fitting that this anniversary is named for one of the hardest and most lasting stones known. 'Diamond' literally means 'unconquerable'. Just as a diamond's sparkle is unsurpassed, so too, we may suppose, is the 'light' reflected by a couple who have shared everything, both joys and sorrows, for so long. Think for a moment, too, of the fact that a diamond is not naturally beautiful. It needs to be worked on at length to become so – just as a good marriage is not the result of 'luck' but of constant effort and attention.

Sixty years of togetherness can serve as a real inspiration to those around the couple, and teach many young marrieds valuable lessons about tolerance, companionship and respect.

Gift suggestions

These should be quite self-evident! To quote the long-running slogan of the famous De Beer's Diamonds, "Diamonds are forever ..."

As tides of time in prospect ebb and flow,
And sands of time drift thither and beyond,
So comes the zenith of life's folio
That few survive to sanction and respond.

Old age, relentless as the sands of time,
Sifts memories of fortitude or tears,
And readily is sorrow set aside,
With recollections of contented years.

For time bestows an amnesty on care,
And with remembrance, life's tenure remains,
While thanksgiving is murmured with a prayer,
And memories of gladness, life sustains.

Len Green

ACKNOWLEDGMENTS / CREDITS

Scripture quotations are from The New King James Version of the Bible, copyright © 1982 by Thomas Nelson Inc. Used by permission. Sincere thanks to Len Green for allowing us to reproduce his poem and to Beverley Cottee for the use of her verse. All efforts have been made to contact the copyright owners of the material in this book. Where this has not been possible, the Publishers invite the persons concerned to contact them.

Purl Harbour; Bondi NSW, Country Trader; Paddington, Potter Williams; Pyrmont NSW, Flower Factory; Nth Sydney NSW, Sweet Art; Paddington NSW, Paraphernalia; Sydney NSW, Sloane's; Paddington NSW, Bald Rock Hotel; Balmain NSW, The Bay Tree; Woollahra NSW, Prima Cosa; Balmain NSW, Glitzi Gifts; Rozelle NSW, Parterre Garden; Woollahra NSW, Linen & Lace; Balmain NSW, Five Way Fusion; Paddington NSW, Nerylla's Antiques; Cammeray NSW, Dinosaur Designs; Paddington NSW, Waterford and Wedgewood at David Jones; Sydney NSW, Michael Green Antiques; Woollahra NSW, Hardy Brothers; Sydney NSW, Sydney Aquarium; Darling Harbour NSW, Percy Marks; Sydney NSW, Jacobus; Woollahra NSW, Boyac, Paddington NSW, Gordon Herford Jewellery Design; Sydney NSW

An Angus & Robertson Publication

Angus&Robertson, an imprint of
HarperCollins *Publishers*
25 Ryde Road, Pymble NSW 2073, Australia
31 View Road, Glenfield, Auckland 10, New Zealand
77–85 Fulham Palace Road, London W6 8JB, United Kingdom
10 East 53rd Street, New York NY 10022, USA
First published in Australia in 1995

National Library of Australia
Cataloguing-in-Publication data:
Brasch, R. (Rudolph), 1912-
The Book of Anniversaries.
ISBN 0 207 18509 3
1. Wedding anniversaries – Miscellanea. I. Title.
392.5

Photography by Nigel Cox Styling by Tim Elkington
Design by Katie Ravich
Printed in Hong Kong

9 8 7 6 5 4 3 2 1
97 96 95

Linen Lace Jewellery Glass or Crystal China Silver Pearl Coral Ruby Sapphire G
len Iron or Sugar Woollen Bronze, Rubber, Salt or Electrical Appliances Copper or
l Ruby Sapphire Golden Emerald Diamond Paper or Plastic Cotton or Calico Leathe
iances Copper or Pottery Aluminium or Tin Steel Linen Lace Jewellery Glass or Cr
on or Calico Leather Silk, or Fruit and Flowers Wooden Iron or Sugar Woollen Bro
Jewellery Glass or Crystal China Silver Pearl Coral Ruby Sapphire Golden Emer
or Sugar Woollen Bronze, Rubber, Salt or Electrical Appliances Copper or Pottery Alu
hire Golden Emerald Diamond Paper or Plastic Cotton or Calico Leather Silk, or F
er or Pottery Aluminium or Tin Steel Linen Lace Jewellery Glass or Crystal China
o Leather Silk, or Fruit and Flowers Wooden Iron or Sugar Woollen Bronze, Rubber,
s or Crystal China Silver Pearl Coral Ruby Sapphire Golden Emerald Diamond
len Bronze, Rubber, Salt or Electrical Appliances Copper or Pottery Aluminium or T
en Emerald Diamond Paper or Plastic Cotton or Calico Leather Silk, or Fruit and F
ttery Aluminium or Tin Steel Linen Lace Jewellery Glass or Crystal China Silver
her Silk, or Fruit and Flowers Wooden Iron or Sugar Woollen Bronze, Rubber, Salt or
ystal China Silver Pearl Coral Ruby Sapphire Golden Emerald Diamond Paper or
ze, Rubber, Salt or Electrical Appliances Copper or Pottery Aluminium or Tin Steel
ald Diamond Paper or Plastic Cotton or Calico Leather Silk, or Fruit and Flowers W
inium or Tin Steel Linen Lace Jewellery Glass or Crystal China Silver Pearl Coral
uit and Flowers Wooden Iron or Sugar Woollen Bronze, Rubber, Salt or Electrical Ap
a Silver Pearl Coral Ruby Sapphire Golden Emerald Diamond Paper or Plastic C
er, Salt or Electrical Appliances Copper or Pottery Aluminium or Tin Steel Linen La
ond Paper or Plastic Cotton or Calico Leather Silk, or Fruit and Flowers Wooden Iron
n Steel Linen Lace Jewellery Glass or Crystal China Silver Pearl Coral Ruby Sa
Flowers Wooden Iron or Sugar Woollen Bronze, Rubber, Salt or Electrical Appliances